THE TRUTH ABOUT LOVE

by   Musea King

© 2002 Musea King

TO SHEILA

who turned my winter into spring, and filled my days with sunshine...

PREFACE

If God is all-powerful, and the whole of creation was planned, He must have expected imperfections at the start.

We can only guess at the reasons for all the pain and suffering human beings have known, but we do know that in a perfect world, everyone would have love in their hearts, instead of anger and hate. There would be no more wars, no more theft or homicide, no more persecution, no more broken relationships, no more starving, and no more lonely people in the world.

The poet Wordsworth said, "Trailing clouds of glory do we come from God who is our home." If we were free to carry the innocence and trust of the new-born child into later life, and so leave a legacy of love to following generations, love for ourselves and others could go on and on till the end of time.

Copyright 2002

LOGIC AND THE TRUTH

Human beings were given the power of logic to find and perceive the truth. Politicians fall when the truth is denied. We lose our respect for those who deceive, and they sometimes end up in gaol.

We are never happy when we conceal the truth. It festers inside like a cancer within, and wrecks our peace of mind.

Many alcoholics conceal the truth from themselves. They think they are badly treated, when they are the worst offenders.

Society itself denies the truth, when it claims that money is everything, and nothing else is needed to make people happy.

The truth is that money is merely a means to live, while true happiness comes from being 'in love' with one's partner. True love is a gift which comes to everyone without warning, and is totally free.

There can surely be no better proof, if proof were needed, that God is a loving God.

BAD TIMES

As a boy I was second to none in class, but I had no social life and very few friends. My teachers advised against the youth club in town, which posed a threat to my studies, and so I was groomed remorselessly for academic 'success'. The fact that my parents were always at war, making me angry inside, and very depressed, didn't matter at all.

My breakdown came the year I was twenty-one. The traditional 'key to the door' was ironic indeed, as my brain was so badly scrambled, I couldn't read a line from a newspaper, let alone a Shakespearean sonnet.

I somehow began to function again, my anger sealed in with pills. But I developed a need for alcohol, and became its slave for twenty-five years. I married the sweetest lady there is, but gave her and our two fine sons a terrible time. Yet to the outside world I was an 'angel', self-effacing and polite, despite the anger bubbling deep inside.

Anger deepens and hardens over the years, but counselling and the programme of Alcoholics Anonymous finally brought it to the surface. I'd fallen in love, and suddenly I seemed to be worth something more than the 'doormat' I'd always been...

As I came off my pills the anger inside exploded. I could take no more being taken for granted, so I quit my job, abandoned my wife and two sons, and headed for pastures new, hoping to find a home and a job in Scotland.

As luck would have it my money ran out, I became homeless, and was forced to return to England. After three months living from hand to mouth, sleeping in shop doorways, bus shelters, meadows and fields, I had a succession of manic attacks, for which I was treated in hospital with pills. A year on out of hospital I am still on medication, mild though it is, to prevent any further attacks.

All I ever craved as a boy was a little love. All I ever got was pills.

THE BEAUTY OF LOVE

A famous general once described an army on the march as "soul extinct, stomach well alive."

When we extract as many O- and A-levels from our children as we can, and make money and 'success' their only goals, where is the difference from an army on the march? Where is the LOVE, and how do our children find it?

Surely it is more important to be successful in love, the one thing which offers lasting happiness and fulfilment. 'Success' in anything else is relative and short-lived. We always crave for more.

Everyone 'falls in love' around the age of puberty, a love which would last and last if given the chance. When we choose for ourselves in later life, a failure rate of 50% is hardly a happy prospect for our young.

The chief obstacles to pubic love are homework, which takes up so much time, parental disapproval, and a law relating to sex which is contrary to our natural instincts. Sadly also, no-one talks about love any more, only SEX, which should come at the end of courtship and NOT the beginning!

True love is, of course, diffusive, and reaches out to help any victim of cruelty or injustice. It abhors fox-hunting and any sport which draws its satisfaction from its cruelty, and it deplores the fact there are so many homeless on our streets, and so many starving round the world.

Without love we are little more than machines, trapped by the money obsession, and going about our daily business with hardly a thought for anyone else. The beauty of love is that it liberates and transforms, and takes away all thought of self. I know a man who was saved from his alcohol addiction by his love for a cat called Smokey. He now has four contented cats who must be the best-loved cats in the world!

I don't doubt that the love which comes with puberty is more than mere coincidence. I am equally sure that such

love comes to everyone on our planet, and if taken up
and taken seriously, would lead to a happy, healthy
carefree world.

BEYOND THE BLUE HORIZON

Falling in love and coming off pills was like lifting a cloud, and for once I felt truly alive. I set out on walks far and wide, and shed many tears as my feelings came through. I felt joy and delight at being in love, but despair at my situation, as so much stood in the way. We both were married with children...

Walking gets the blood flowing. I'd narrowly escaped a by-pass after a heart attack, but after two years of walking I had a check-up in Glasgow, and was roundly rebuked for wasting their time. I promptly threw my heart pills away, and haven't taken one since.

Walking also soothes the mind and refreshes the soul. The ever-changing landscape, as new scenes unfold, is a constant inspiration, which lures the traveller on to more and more unseen delights.

So the sights and sounds of nature gave me comfort as I wandered on in hope that someday my love would succeed.

Although I've been ill, I hope to go on my walks again soon. The love I craved has passed me by, but the paths and bye-ways beneath my feet are there throughout the land, and maybe someday I'll find a pot of gold beyond the blue horizon...

'BOOTS'

I love my walking boots. They're cracked across the instep and almost bust in two, they've been caked with mud, drenched with rain and twice repaired, but I love my walking boots.

They took me everywhere without complaint, first to familiar places close to home: Long Melford, Sudbury, Haverhill, Thetford, Stowmarket, Lavenham and Mildenhall, and many villages too.

Then they accompanied me on long-distance trails, the Icknield Way, the Peddars Way, the Angles Way and the Stour Valley River Path. Rising next to the challenge, they strode the dales of Derbyshire, and many fine sights we saw.

Now with the bit between our teeth, we went straight on to Scotland, attempting the West Highland Way. We walked from Milngavie to Killearn, from Drymen to Balmaha, and strolled along the beautiful 'Bonny Banks' of Loch Lomond. Straight up Ben Lomond we climbed, more than 3000 feet, straining and panting, with not one slip or stumble all the way, and resting the night half-way down. On we went to Fort William by bus, and testing every sinew and nerve, we stood at length on the summit of Ben Nevis itself.

On a later visit we took the Corran Ferry, and with occasional lifts we walked the remote Ardnamurchan peninsular, crossing by boat to Tobermory on the Isle of Mull, and returning by bus and ferry to the beautiful town of Oban.

My boots have tramped the streets of Glasgow and trekked from town to town in Suffolk, Essex and Cambridgshire, when I was homeless in search of lodging.

Since I was ill they've taken a rest. They pinch my toes and the leather is too far gone, so I'm planning to purchase new.

I'd been kicked around for 40 odd years, but my boots helped shake the dust off my feet, when I was low and alone...

I shall never part with my boots!

To David Blunkett MP What is the PURPOSE of education?

Is it to soak in as much information as possible like a sponge, and squeeze it all out at the end in tests or exams - regardless of whether it is relevant to one's needs in later life?

Or is it to locate and develop a child's NATURAL aptitudes, so that what he learns will stick, and probably be useful in later life?

Or are charts and league tables all that really matter these days, so that teachers can say, as in the comedy programme:

Didn't we do well! ??

Surely the learning years of our children should be treated with somewhat more care and respect than is accorded to a game of FOOTBALL, with a "winners and losers" credo behind it all.

With the proper approach every child would be a winner, given the attention by teachers to his specific needs and APTITUDES, which vary widely from one child to another. Some will one day be doctors, nurses, scientists and so on. But there will be others who will be happy to work on a dustcart collecting refuse, or on the production line in a factory or the check-out in a store, or in some capacity on a building site, etc etc. Does it really make SENSE for this group to sweat at their studies right up to the age of 16, when most or all of it will be gone from memory and never referred to again soon after they have left the school gates behind with a huge sigh of relief?

Many may do quite well in their final exams, but if what they learn with great effort will never be used and mostly quite quickly forgotten, whatever is the point of it all, other than to make a contribution to the teachers' league table stakes, which seems rather a hollow reward for all that effort.

Of course the three R's should be taught as usual, after which the interesting and rewarding part should follow, as children discover what they are good at and follow it up accordingly. But we do not need, nor should we have, pressurised education, with children taking on as many subjects as they possibly can, and taking home piles of homework every day, while teachers worry themselves to breaking point over silly league tables and statistics. Someone sometime is going to have to draw the line and say enough is enough.

Learning should be a joy and a pleasure for all involved, not a mad scramble to collect as many medals as possible in some kind of race, which is all over and done with at the end of school or college, when everyone can say farewell to learning and thank goodness the ORDEAL is all over.

"The God of Efficiency"

We spend a fortune on our luckless children, in the pressure-cooker environment of school and college to achieve arbitrary levels of attainment in artificial tests within an arbitrary timescale, at a supposedly 'crucial' time in their lives, with the sole object, it would appear, of chalking up as many academic "pars", "birdies" or "eagles" as any golfer might hope to obtain after a year or two of practice on his local course.

The lucky golfer knows full well that for him it is just a game which he can play any time, win or lose, any day or whenever for the rest of his life, and that as with life itself, he will sometimes fail to meet the goals he sets himself. Sadly, the unlucky child or student, with little experience of adult cunning or subterfuge, nor any knowledge of the insane pressures often applied to the teachers themselves to get "results", may well come to the inescapable but spurious conclusion that "success" in achieving the requisite target, given the insistent emphasis and importance attached to it by parents and teachers alike, is an essential prerequisite for any kind of happiness or "success" in later life.

Many of course will say that this is a gross exaggeration and distortion of the truth, which perhaps for many it is. I am sure, nevertheless, that for many others, especially where fear of parental disapproval or displeasure has been sown in the home, fear of failure will begin to take root and grow in the young child's mind as a gratuitous and unwelcome by-product of the "system".

The underlying fear is surely that "failure" may well invite the misery of even more morale-damaging reprimands or pressures to "do better" from well meaning but often misguided parents or teachers, whose own training and upbringing has led them to be insensitive to the child's overriding need for unconditional love and approval, however well or badly he performs a particular task, which forms the mainspring and foundation for the growth of trust and the ability to feel and express love for others in later life.

It is not surprising, therefore, that many of our young succumb to the pressure, to join the flood of victims who make up the growing stream of misery which flows through the corridors of our hospital wards of shame, bearing the emotive label of "mentally sick". Quite simply they have been savagely traumatised into a state of acute anxiety and depression, as was the writer himself many years past, by the insane, exorbitant demands and expectations of a society which itself is "mentally sick" in so far it has become so obsessed with the need for "output" or "efficiency" from its members that other, more vital needs are swept to one side or ignored in the stampede for "success". Many children must feel that the price for love and security is a never-ending assault course repeated later in the workplace, in a world where love only comes at a price, if it ever truly comes at all!

So long as our children are treated like cattle in a pen, or horses in a race, or statistics on a chart so long will succeeding generations of children suffer the same. So long as we place the god of efficiency before the God of Love, and before love for one another, the sad truth is we will never be "efficient" at making people "happy" in society as we know it today, in fact quite the opposite. It is a statistical fact as I write that Esther Rantzen's childline receives more than 10,000 calls for help every day, of which only around 3000 are answered through lack of volunteers. It is also a fact that more than three million citizens are receiving treatment for depression in Britain at any given time. It is also sadly true that deaths from suicide are now as numerous as deaths on our roads. Does not all of this add up to an unacceptable and appalling pile of misery of almost holocaust proportions which we cannot and must not ignore any longer?

Paradoxically, there is nothing wrong with efficiency as such. I like it when my bus turns up on time. I am annoyed, as anyone, if I buy a product which fails to function properly or falls to pieces for no good reason. It is only when "efficiency at any price" (or as the top priority) becomes the norm that things go seriously wrong. For example, it appears to be widely acknowledged within the teaching profession, that so much fear and insecurity has been generated by pressures for greater efficiency in recent years, that many have been falling out and leaving their jobs through "stress" or "stress related" illness. From a wider viewpoint who, I wonder, takes into account the aftermath for all these victims, whose talents and years of expensive training have now been rendered useless, not to mention the needs of any dependents for whom the "breadwinner" is now out of action? Who foots the bill for the highly paid teams of skilled and qualified doctors, psychiatrists and social workers or counsellors whose services are now required in response to each new victim's "health problem", not forgetting the armies of welfare administrators who are needed to ascertain and supply, with laborious precision, the state support which is due to the victim and his dependents. It doesn't take a genius in mathematics to work out the bottom-line figure in all of that! - all for the sake of a bit more "efficiency" in the classroom?!

Is it not a fact that a little "milk of human kindness", instead of the usual "milk of magnesia" remedies for rough treatment, might just make life, in time, a lot more palatable, and even enable most of us to stomach change, when it comes, with ease and equanimity? Who knows, we might even one day stop for ever seeking shelter and start chasing rainbows again like we did as children, when love and laughter was all around us, and "to be young was very Heaven!"

LOST AND GONE FROM MEMORY

It is strange how quickly one forgets all or most that one learns at school. Memory is a fickle thing, but after imbibing huge amounts of information, I have to state that little was retained after leaving school.

There were many things I would like to have done as a boy, but homework always seemed to get in the way. Having a breakdown was the price I paid for taking the pressure too seriously. But then, I was only a boy.

Many teachers have been falling apart with breakdowns because of the pressure to pack the kids' brains with more and more. But I suspect that for accuracy, volume and durability, the computer beats the brain every time.

Sadly we cannot do much about that, though government ministers would be over the moon if they could!

I can recall a few bits and pieces of what I learned, mainly English, my favourite subject. But Physics is just a black hole in memory, while all I recall of Chemistry is playing around with test tubes and bunsen burner, creating nasty smells about the place!

As for those horrid exams, what would be wrong with a teacher's report and a simple IQ test, for goodness sake?!

AND SO TO BED

Some people think the homeless put themselves on the street.

They couldn't be more wrong. Sometimes they have to leave home when a relationship fails, and the spouse claims income support. They may be out of work, and have no money for rent or bed and breakfast accommodation.

Sometimes they are ejected from the home by an angry parent. Sometimes, in desperation, they flee the home of disturbed and violent parents, despite having nowhere to go. I met a young man who left home because he feared for his life.

Sometimes they cannot keep up with the rent and eventually are evicted, a common cause.

No-one forsakes a nice warm bed for a cold, hard pavement without good cause.

Some treat the homeless with open contempt, which compounds the cruel injustice of their situation.

The DSS is supposed to provide a safety net. In my case it just wasn't there. Homes and hostels were full everywhere. There wasn't sufficient support.

And still we accept that some every year will die from the cold.

You could call it death by misadventure. I call it corporate manslaughter, by a sick, self-seeking society which has lost its soul...

A SOCIAL PARIAH

I was homeless in Cambridge, the place where once as a boy I'd applied for a college place.

It was bitterly cold, with a chilling wind that took your breath away. There was frost in the air, and you could feel it nipping your fingers and toes.

I walked along the Victoria road, looking for somewhere away from the wind where I wouldn't be disturbed. At length I came across a small hospital, with lights inside and beckoning double doors.

I thought, if only they would let me in and let me sleep in some corner or box-room away from the wind. But I knew it was hopeless. Hospitals are not for the homeless. I turned away and found a small patch of grass, beneath some trees in the hospital grounds, hoping no-one would see me and move me on.

I had two pairs of trousers and extra socks to keep me warm in my sleeping bag. I was luckier than some, no doubt, that night. The trees were handy if I should have a call of nature, as the public loo was always shut at night.

In the morning I was up and away like a frightened rabbit, as I knew that I was trespassing. I walked a mile or so to the shops to buy a cold drink and a sandwich, and waited for the loo to open. I managed to get a wash and a shave, but the water was icy cold.

Then I waited to start my job selling newspapers at a roadside kiosk. I was desperately tired, which seemed to annoy my boss, but I don't think there were any other contenders, as the money wasn't too good.

Sometimes I slept in the multi-story car-park, with cars going by till the early hours. At least it was out of the wind.

I was none too keen to be homeless - a blot on the landscape and a social pariah struggling to survive...

HELP, I AM HOMELESS!

I was pleased so many rushed to my aid when sadly I was made homeless. My friends shed crocodile tears and fondly waved goodbye. My wife said I shouldn't be in the marital home, now that we were separated, and she was on income support. The DSS refused a crisis loan and referred me to a home for the homeless which was full. A lady from Citizens Advice recommended a place which was all locked up, as the management were on holiday. My financial adviser advised he couldn't arrange a loan on the strength of my house, because I was out of work.

That was when I saw red. There is nothing like anger to get the feet moving, and I desperately wanted away from the township I'd lived in for twenty-five years. I was 58, and after a lifetime in work I had nothing. I was destitute, homeless, and shunned by my own community.

The one saving grace was the sick note my doctor gave, which meant I'd have some money to live, if I could cope until it came through. In addition my wife let me have £10, which kept me going on bread and jam and orange squash until my money arrived.

Ironically, I was planning to take on temporary work at the time, but was told I wouldn't get dole for at least eight days, which was too late for my needs.

Luckily I had a rucksack and sleeping bag, which kept me alive for the next few months, searching for lodging everywhere, until my head gave in and I was taken to hospital with the first of five manic attacks.

Life is full of 'ifs' at the best of times. If the support had been there at the start, such as dole money straight away, or a crisis loan, I might have secured a job, a place to live and an acceptable quality of life.

Yet the journey had its rewards. I'd never experienced manic attacks before, the claustrophobia of hospital care with freedom denied, nor the grim realities of living on the street.

I now have a beautiful flat, with caring neighbours, in a quiet corner of town. I have time to write, which has become a labour of love, and I can go for walks whenever I please.

I no longer crave for money, as I have sufficient to cope, and I don't need the luxury of a car, which I can manage well without.

But above all I'm a wiser, happier man than ever I was, and, I hope, a better person too.

———————————

SECURITY AND MENTAL ILLNESS

When I was first taken to hospital, no-one at any time questioned me about the events leading up to my admission. The fact is I'd been homeless for three months immediately prior to hospitalisation, and the hospital bed was the first bed I'd slept in for a considerable time. It was also the first time in weeks I'd had a proper cooked meal. One should also appreciate that living on the street generates acute anxiety, especially as winter approaches! So fear and insecurity were instrumental in making me ill.

Another patient I met had been caring for his sickly parents. He pleaded for help from social services, but none was forthcoming, and so he became ill with the worry. Two other patients I met had lost their jobs, and couldn't find a replacement. They too had become desperately anxious and fallen ill. An older man had gone out of his mind with worry after losing his job and repeatedly failing to find another.

Another young man who had parted from his wife and four young children had been advised by his solicitor to give up his job and live on social security, as he couldn't afford the maintenance. I think he went crazy with anger and frustration!

There were others, of course, whose security had been threatened or destroyed by the break-up of a relationship, and anxiety again had led to dementia.

So worry and fear have a large part to play in the causes of mental illness, and the breakdown of family life and high unemployment are often to blame.

BOVINE MEDICATION - A WORM'S EYE VIEW

Every time I had a manic attack, the doctors plied me with heavy-duty anti-psychotic drugs, which to my mind I didn't need once I was back to normal.

My attacks only lasted a few days, and yet I spent eight long months in a Granta home on pills which reduced me to a nervous wreck. In my experience, all sedatives tend to induce feelings of nervousness, and when you sit with doctors and nurses at a formal meeting you tend to feel 'on trial', as you know your freedom is on the line!

Some patients I met were so full of drugs they were more like cattle than worthwhile, dynamic human beings, with CPN's and social workers more in the role of herdsmen than anything else. This is not to say it is anyone's fault, nor to detract from the work the social workers and CPN's do.

But counselling early on, with a speedy withdrawal from drugs, would surely be a better approach, conducive to a happier outcome. The real, emotional origins of the illness could then be located and dealt with for good.

No-one wants to be a zombie in a semi-comatose state for years, running on two cylinders instead of four, which is all I was for twenty-five years while on Stelazine.

SIDE EFFECTS

It's the medication that makes the muscles move in your legs so you cannot stand still, and you dance to and fro all day without rest.

It's the medication that gives you pain in your legs when you walk. Walking used to be a delight, but now it is just an ordeal.

It's the medication that makes you panic whenever you come under stress. People think it's the illness, but it's the godamm medication.

It's the medication that makes you drowsy much of the time. You think you are lazy, as everything seems such an effort. You are not really lazy at all, it's the wretched medication.

It's the medication that takes your libido away along with your courage too. It's not the illness at all, but simply the medication.

It's the medication which blocks you off from your feelings, leaving you numb inside like a block of wood, with no hope of getting well.

And so you are labelled disabled, not so much by the illness as by the vicious, obscene medication.

But it's best to stay on the stuff, as the withdrawals can be horrific, and without skilled help you are likely to 'flip' again!

'CHEMICAL IMBALANCE'

I don't doubt that feelings are reflected in body chemistry, and that the so-called 'chemical imbalance' in the brain is due to negative feelings inside, especially anger and fear. Such feelings may go right back to childhood, and a few simple questions may quickly reveal the source of the problem.

A child deprived of love tends to withdraw into himself, and his anger may lie hidden for years, growing in strength until some stressful situation arises and makes him ill. My own parents were always at war when I was a boy, which made me angry and depressed. In my case the anger all went inwards, and only dispersed when I finally forgave my deceased father, with help from the programme of Alcoholics Anonymous.

I know I did terrible harm to my children, but at least I can offer them love now instead of hate, knowing that love is the greatest healer of all.

Love at the right time, early in life, is the finest insurance against ill health, and being 'in love' with one's partner is in my view the key to a happy and lasting relationship, giving love and security to the children, and a firm base for their future.

'Truelove' comes to everyone around the age of puberty, but education, finding a job, and saving for a home all seem to come first, so it seldom succeeds.

Most illness, in my belief, is due to a lack of love, and professional 'care' would not be necessary in a happy, loving society.

———————————

EMPLOYMENT - A CRUEL SITUATION

It is perhaps worth noting that in 1961 there were 250,000 unemployed in England. At the time of writing in 2002 there are a million on the dole. Which means for every two people who applied for a job in 1961 there are now eight. Consequently those of our longterm sick who are persuaded to try for a job, have little hope of success, with so many fit and healthy people in the running. In 1961 you could get a job just like that, even if you were, like myself, being treated for a mental illness. And employers were anxious to hold on to their staff, which made them feel secure.

But as we all know, it is a different scene today, with draconian pressures applied to staff in many places of work, and many, such as teachers, wilting and falling ill with the stress.

Statutory measures to reduce the working week would help take up the slack in the dole queue, and ultimately relieve the pressure on employees and job-seekers alike, at the same time reducing the burden on the NHS and social services.

The only thing that stands in the way of change is the moronic obsession with money. Yet the community as a whole would benefit, with lower health costs, less dole money to find, less bureaucracy, and, with fewer people out of work, less crime.

I can remember a time when people left their doors unlocked at night, and the word 'mugging' hadn't been invented.

It's a pity that politicians have tunnel vision...

THE TRUTH ABOUT UNEMPLOYMENT

Human beings, of course, are naturally lazy. You see it in the young, skipping and jumping up and down and forever asking their Mums what they can do next.

You see it in the unemployment figures too, with a huge rise from 250,000 in 1961 to 1.7 million in 1999, which suggests that laziness gets even worse as the years go by. No wonder there's been such a decline in industry in the north. No-one wants to work, so they just can't recruit the staff...

Of course there are sanctions and penalties, where people appear not to want to work - perhaps they just missed the bus to an interview - but then they just turn to crime, which suits them better, as they can do it when they please.

In some parts, of course, they work like slaves and are actually fearful of losing their jobs. But that, of course, is only because they happen to have a mortgage and payments on a car to keep up. If they could they would far sooner give up the lot and get a council house and live on the dole for the rest of their days. Who needs holidays away, nice clothes, a car, and a pint down the pub now and then?

The TRUTH is that unemployment rises in inverse proportion to the number of jobs available.

So paranoid pressures on those out of work can only serve to increase their misery and frustration!

———————————

THE LONELY HOME

Women have been schooled and hardened to forsake their motherly role in the home, and take their place in the workplace.

Children suffer, of course, but no-one seems to mind. As long as they get a 'full and rounded' education, which is their 'right', or conversely their obligation, it doesn't matter at all.

Parents and teachers seldom stop to ask the children if they enjoy the learning process. Examinations are stressful, but only for the child. Parents and teachers can wait to applaud or commiserate at their leisure. It's a race to the finish, with the nagging suspicion that if you should fail you are 'finished' once and for all.

It's easy to see why some of our young commit suicide) with family breakdown and pressurised education combining to bring them down. Of course with Mum out at work, Dad gone off, and grandma stuck in the 'home', there's no-one to hear their anger and hurt, or that lonely voice inside.

But that doesn't matter. As long as Mum can keep in work and keep the economy going, it doesn't matter a damn. There's no time to deal with children's feelings, and the only hearing they get is before the magistrates when they misbehave. Output and efficiency are everything, and the way you feel is nothing to anyone.

Women traditionally are the main source of goodness and love. Without love we are nothing...

FAMILY(?)LIFE

Mother works like a bee all day, as the shop is always full. Then she has the shopping to do, chasing around with an eye to bargain prices. Near exhausted, she gets home at last to cook the evening meal, not forgetting the washing that needs to be done, and the washing up after the meal.

Then there's Junior fretting over his homework. He needs attention too, and hubby is griping as usual over the pressures of his job.

Sometimes she wonders if the extra car is worth it, holidays away and the best food money can buy. If she gave up her job, granny could come out of the home, and her pension would be of some help. She could give more attention to Junior, and help more with hubby's moods. They wouldn't need the extra car, as the ·shops aren't far away.

But then there's the mortgage. Shame that the proceeds of granny's house all went off to the home. Shame they didn't take her in- she could have cleared the mortgage.

But then who could look after granny, when you've a job to do all day, to pay for the extra car, help with the mortgage, and holidays away?...

Who needs grannies anyway?...

THE HEART OF THE FAMILY

We love our gran. She sits in the chair and keeps an eye on all of us. She makes sure we keep the windows shut when it's cold, and open when it's warm. We don't mind her telling us what to do. She makes demands, but we made demands of her. She had a household to run for years and years, running around to get meals, ironing clothes, shopping for food and all the rest. She was always there when needed. Now we are there for her. We love our gran, and she loves us too.

Down the road is the old people's home. They sit there and stare, waiting to die. It's a far cry from home, with little real love to keep them warm. Some are still lively, but many feel the loneliness deep inside. No-one can ease that inner pain of not being needed, existing for the sake of no-one in particular) left to patiently wither away, time passing slowly with each laborious hour, day after day, night after night in palpable silence.

There are thousands huddled in homes away from home, waiting to die.

Gran is up to her tricks again, trying to walk when we all know she musn't in case she should fall. And she will keep telling us what to do.

But we really don't mind. We'll be the same one day. Besides, we wouldn't even be here if it wasn't for gran...

SOMEONE TO COME HOME TO

Two can get by better than one. In a crisis, such as a gas leak or power cut, you can lean on each other for support, swap suggestions and quickly make light of it all. When you are the only one there's no-one to turn to to share your worries, except for a neighbour perhaps, who may not be that much concerned.

People naturally live in family groups, the same as the apes, and never should live alone.

It's nice to have someone to come home to, someone with whom you can share the day's events, if only to say that potatoes are up in price, and there's no more bread in the shops. If there's no-one to report to or talk to, what kind of life is that? Who cares that you couldn't get any bread? Who cares that potatoes are up in price? The walls can't talk, nor can the empty chairs...

The other day an elderly lady in town fell down and broke her leg. She lay there alone for three whole days, before help finally came. It happens all the time. Luckily she survived...

A friend informed me whenever he gets a bill through the door he loses two nights' sleep. Yet he KNOWS he has the money to pay. He happens to live alone...

A child has a nasty fall in the playground. Teacher rings her Mum at work. She says she can't get away, but should be home by five. Teacher frowns and the girl hobbles home in pain.

It's nice to have someone to come home to...

LOVE LIES BLEEDING

Boy meets girl and they fall in love. He is sixteen and she is only twelve. He was slow but she was fast in reaching puberty. Neither has been with anyone before.

Their love develops quite quickly, as they see each other every day. A few months on it comes to the point where they long to consummate, and he buys some condoms, as she is too young for children, but cannot obtain the pill. They love each other so much they would like to shout it to the heavens!

Mother finds out what is going on and is horrified in the extreme. She places her daughter under house arrest, and you'd think the sky had blown in...

He is 'of age' and 'should have known better', so he goes to gaol to cool his heels and his ardour.

Dad says he'd rather not see him again as she's only a slut of a girl, and Mum hangs her head in shame.

That's how we LOVE our young these days...

PUBIC LOVE

If the animals of the forest, the birds of the air, the fish in the waters, the bees and all the myriad insect life on earth, are allowed to mate as soon as they are sexually mature, why do we stamp on pubic love, the most wonderful and inspiring experience a young person can have, as though it were worthless?

I have spoken to many people, and they can all remember their first romantic love as though it were yesterday. Falling in love has to be the most beautiful, uplifting and happy experience known to man.
It crosses all boundaries - race, colour, creed and social status,- and literally lights up the lives of those who receive it.

It comes to all around the age of puberty, and once formed it never dies. So where is the sanity in imposing an arbitrary 'age of consent' on a natural, healthy instinct which usually occurs before the law allows?(?)

I can only assume it is deliberately held back(?) to coincide with completion of O-levels in schools.

Unfortunately by that time the opportunity is usually lost and gone, and most boys and girls have to make do with a less than perfect relationship based on physical attraction or infatuation and nothing more.

If we trample on God's gift of love we must reap the consequences, with 50% of relationships falling apart, and a huge amount of attendant misery for everyone involved...

ABORTIVE EXPEDITION

I went to a disco a while ago, but I couldn't get into the feel of the place. Men were dancing and clasping the ladies' bums, but I never got into the feel of the place.

I tried to make conversation at times, but the music was all I could hear. Perhaps if I'd brought a hearing aid it wouldn't have been such a strain. I just couldn't get into the feel of the place.

I slipped between the shuffling feet and had the odd beer from the bar. At least I could hear the barman as he sang out the price and made it abundantly clear.

There were whizzing lights all over the place, to help you see in the dark, but you couldn't see too well at all, close up or afar. I just couldn't get into the feel of the place.

There were some women showing their breasts and some their thighs, which gave a vicarious thrill. One man kindly said that I'd soon get to know them all, but how or whereby I couldn't be really sure. I just couldn't get into the feel of the place.

I quite like music, and most sorts too, but the pounding in my ears of the disco din was too much in the end.

And so I left.

PROMISCUITY AND 'RABBITS'

Promiscuity is a foolish and dangerous pastime. Boys should have more respect and girls more sense. AIDS is a killer disease, now rated among the top five, along with cancer and heart disease.

Feelings also are frequently hurt, and great harm is done by clandestine relationships when the truth comes out.

Human beings are much more than rabbits, or should be, with a great capacity for love. When love and sex combine the result is perfect bliss, not for an hour or a day, but the whole of one's lifetime to come.

The old-fashioned notion that boys should sow their 'wild oats' is a nonsense. If their first 'true love' in life was successful, there would be no need for 'wild oats' at all!

But no-one places a value on love any more, only money and sex. And so we have a rich society with a huge pile of misery underneath, 50% of relationships breaking down, 30% of the population living alone, 5000 children in 'care', three million being treated for depression at any one time, and child help-lines besieged with calls for help.

It would help if the boys zipped up their trousers, and the girl hitched up their knickers, and waited for true love to come.

Then we would have some real men and women about the place, and society would improve!

REALLY INVOLVED

True love is unconditional. You would lay down your life for the person concerned. Mother love is much like that, or should be, and so is the love we feel when we 'fall in love' with that special person for us.

Care is something else. There are professional carers everywhere, specially trained not to get too involved: doctors, nurses, psychiatrists, social workers, counsellors and the rest, who earn a living from their 'care'. Many are very caring, but it's too dangerous to get involved. You can 'care' for your partner too, of course, but it's still not the same as 'true love'.

In an ideal world I believe we wouldn't need so many carers about the place, with relationships formed on a solid base of true love, and people actively seeking to help one another, instead of thinking only of themselves.

Christian love is like that, with Christ as the perfect example of love, dying on the cross for the sake of those who mocked and condemned Him.

Now we are in the third millennium, it seems to me we have reached a point where change must come soon, before the earth becomes a barren waste, or merely a place where everyone chases money and sex and very little else, and the only creatures you can TRUST are your pets!...

TRUE LOVE

People know when they fall in love. It hits them between the eyes and there's no escape. It's the best feeling there is, and it makes you come alive.

If everyone was aware of the importance of such love, we could soon have a better world, with people giving rather than taking all the time.

All it needs is for parents and teachers to give their support for true love to grow when it comes.

Who needs broken relationships, promiscuous sex like rabbits, when it needn't happen at all? Who needs insecurity, the shock of betrayal, the misery of rejection, when there's never any need? Who needs sexually transmitted disease? Who do you know for sure that's CLEAN when you go out looking for sex? Who wants to go with someone and then get bored and not know what to do? That's when the bickering sets in, when everything starts to go wrong.

True love is never like that. It just goes on and on with a perfect understanding of each other's needs, no jaded days of grey to spoil it all.

It also brings peace of mind and happiness such as you've never known before.

That's what true love is...

A GOD OF LOVE

Some people say there's a hell after death for those who misbehave. If that is the case there cannot be a God of love, for who could bring life to an innocent child, who had no choice in being born, only to condemn him in the end to everlasting pain? No father on earth could wish such a fate for the children he has sired, nor could a loving God.

Nor could a loving God bring forth children in anger and hate. It wouldn't make any sense, for anger is a destructive force, and cannot create at all. When a man and a woman conjoin to produce a child it's an act of love, not of hate.

Many relationships fail because the couple are not 'in love'. One is never too young or too old to receive 'true love', which comes right out of the blue, and is surely a gift from God. Such a glorious gift is surely proof enough that God is a loving God, who would never consign His children to oblivion, let alone hell.

Most people's lives are drab and dull, but true love is never like that. It excites the senses all the time, and nothing can match its splendour, beauty and joy.

Such love never dies once it is formed, so surely we should take it up when it comes, for the greater glory of God and the sake of all mankind.

ADDICTION - THE TRAIN THAT WON'T STOP

The train seemed so comfortable when first you got on.
Soft velvet seat, plenty of room to spread your legs,
The fare was reasonable too.

It started slowly, increasing in speed as the weeks and months rolled by. For some strange reason the train wouldn't stop, it just kept on going, faster and faster as it seemed.

The plush seat was threadbare after a while, the ticket collector wore a frown, and the weather was dark clouds and rain the whole time.

For some strange reason you wanted to stop, yet you wanted to keep on going. You couldn't bear to stop and get off. The train was your life, and YOU were not to blame.

You longed to see your family again without the noise of the train. You had to shout at them all of the time because of the noise of the train. You tried to explain that you NEED the train more than anything else in the world, then said you'd get off as soon as you could.

But the only way of stopping the train is to seek help from God, as there isn't a driver in sight,

We should open our hearts to those in such a plight, and help as best we can...

———————————

MY FATHER

My father used to come downstairs on a Sunday, clad in an old vest full of holes, struggling to clear his chest and spitting into the open fire.

As a small boy I wasn't very impressed with that, but I had no say in the matter! He was a dyed-in-the-wool Victorian, and you didn't speak unless spoken to. Two sayings are etched in my mind, which he never tired of reciting. The first was "silence is golden", and the second "little boys should be seen but not heard!"

. He had an atrocious temper, forever berating my mother and finding fault, which went on all through my childhood, making me angry and insecure. Yet my eldest brother once told me he had an idyllic child hood. He was born and brought up before the war.

I believe the war changed my father, and made him a nervous wreck. German bombers flew directly over the town in wave after wave on their way to London, and my earliest memory is being held in my mother's arms under the kitchen table. Many years later she told me my father was so unnerved he would run to a neighbour's house at the onset of a raid.

He became an insomniac, reading for hours while we all slept. He dare not go in a shop for a packet of cigarettes, and although he continued to work, he became a recluse, avoiding all social gatherings, and gambling on the horses for recreation.

I hated him as a boy, but I don't hate him now. He had a burden to carry not of his making, and I hope we meet up in Heaven some day...

ANGER AND RESENTMENTS

Anger is a painful, uncomfortable feeling, but a perfectly natural one. It comes when the truth or our value as human beings is denied. If our partner is unfaithful we feel angry and misused. If we are thrown out on to the street, we feel angry and abused. If we are bullied at school by bigger boys we get angry as hell as there's no way of fighting back. There's always a reason for anger.

The word 'resent' means to 'feel again'. So a resentment is a feeling of anger which keeps coming back whenever one thinks of the person or persons who caused it. Current resentments are stressful, and always cause misery and pain. If someone upset me I used to seethe for days, unable to let it go. Someone might say something in jest, which touched a sensitive nerve, and the whole thing would escalate in my mind, affecting my sleep, my work and my whole peace of mind.

But the worst resentments of all are deep-rooted ones, which lie out of sight but affect us in every way, casting a shadow over our lives, and often wrecking any real chance of forming a happy and lasting relationship.

To be happy, deep-rooted resentments have to go. We have to forgive the people who hurt us, often one of our parents, totally and completely, so they no longer have a place in our heads. Old resentments deepen and harden over the years. When I came off my pills and did my Step 4 of the programme of Alcoholics Anonymous, I found a huge ball of hate for my deceased father, which I had never acknowledged before, and it was agony just to face and accept that it was there.

Fears go hand in hand with resentments, and I'd lived in fear the whole of my life. I had to pray for my fears and resentments to go, which they did in the course of time. Step nine helped me forgive my father. I wrote a brief letter, saying I was sorry I'd blamed him for everything that went wrong in my life and wishing him peace and joy in Heaven.

That little letter must rate as the most important I ever wrote. The strangest thing, as I came to the end I felt a huge burden was lifted, and I KNEW I'd forgiven my father, and God had forgiven me too.

I can still get angry at times, if the truth is denied, or when I am treated unfairly by others along the way. But the anger quickly subsides. I don't hold on to it any more.

In a perfect world, of course, there would be no need for anger to raise its ugly head. People would give out love, and they wouldn't need to tell lies. Our children would be happy, and when they fell in love they'd be given the chance to see their love succeed.

If we have anger inside we cannot love. To be happy we have to love...

DIDN'T YOU KNOW?

Look at the boy who's a bully at school. Have you never stopped to think why? Have you not peeped through the curtains of his home, to find out what goes on?

Didn't you know his father drinks and is an ex-army man, a strict disciplinarian, cold and cruel, who rules the home with an iron fist? Didn't you know?

Didn't you know that your bully boy hardly dares open his mouth at home? Didn't you know his Mum is always at work, and often he gets his own meals - didn't you know?

Didn't you know his father beats him at times, after he's had a drink? Didn't you know his backside was badly bruised and sore for a week?

Didn't you know?

Didn't you know his sister is father's favourite, and can't do anything wrong? Didn't you know she taunts her brother for being in trouble at school?

Didn't you know?

Didn't you know he is lonely and angry inside, and takes it out on the other kids? Didn't you know?

He is one of our bullies in schools.

I was a bully behind closed doors.

Hitler was beaten by his Dad, and taunted by his peers...

UNLESS IT HAPPENS TO YOU

Drug addicts and alcoholics are the scum of the earth, - unless it happens to you.

People who put their children in care are vermin as well - unless it happens to you.

People who steal when they have no cash are the lowest of the low - unless it happens to you;

The homeless living on our streets are only fit for the dustbin - unless it happens to you.

The mentally sick are weaklings, who should be made to work to toughen them up - unless it happens to you.

It's all their own fault they've been damaged in early life or fallen foul of the system - unless it happens to you.

If you've led a charmed life and always got by, how could you understand- if it's never happened to you?

THERE, BUT FOR THE GRACE OF GOD, GO I...

SIN, GUILT AND FORGIVENESS

The concepts of sin and guilt are as old as mankind itself. When we harm others we always feel guilty afterwards, unless so blinded by hate, we cannot feel the guilt inside.

Anger and hate arise because we are short on love in early life. Forgiving those who failed us and hurt us takes away all the hate, and enables us to love. We also need God's forgiveness, as in the Lord's Prayer, "Forgive us our trespasses, as we forgive those that trespass against us." Then we can forgive ourselves and be at peace and high in self-esteem.

I cannot believe we were born in sin, with hate in our hearts, a notion which flies in the face of the concept of an all-powerful, all-loving God. But life imposes so many pressures and restraints, which hurt and harm us along the way, that we lose the power to love.

Forgiveness all round makes us whole. It is the ninth or 'amends' step of the programme of Alcoholics Anonymous, when the burden of guilt is finally taken away. It is a wonderful feeling, and we feel glad to be alive!

We can still have anger at times, when the truth or our value is denied, but it doesn't last, and we soon forgive and forget. And if we hurt others without thinking, as we all make mistakes at times, we quickly say sorry and make amends, and the feeling of guilt goes away.

So we don't have to wallow in feelings of guilt all our lives. As human beings we have a right to feel good about ourselves, and about life, and to live our lives in happiness, peace and harmony with others.

GOOD SAMARITANS

If life on earth is to improve, a sea-change needs to take place in the way we think about life and our fellow men.

Most of us think about money in an obsessive, self centred way, ignoring the needs of others, just dropping the odd coin here and there into someone's charity box, to ease the pricks of conscience.

It would take just a tiny cut in wages and profits throughout the civilised world, to give the homeless a home, and to feed all those who starve. Human beings are the greatest asset we have, and the potential spending power of the under-developed nations must be enormous.

If sufficient funds were applied, with technical support, the impoverished third world states could one day be rich like ourselves, and ourselves even richer through the increase in trade. From a global point of view, the civilised world has everything to gain by giving some of its wealth to make the whole world wealthy.

The problem with money is that nobody wants to part with it. We want it only for ourselves. Of course there are exceptions, but there aren't enough Good Samaritans to cope with global poverty, and unscrupulous business-men simply exploit the scene.

There is nothing wrong with the profit motive, as long as we pay due care to the welfare of others, the same way we care for ourselves.

So a richer world, with security for all, is not a pipe-dream beyond our reach, as long as we put people first, and focus on the world as a whole, not just our own share of the cake. Increase in trade increases the wealth of all involved, so our '.share' would increase accordingly.

But one has to give to get a return. The Good Samaritan laid out his money for his enemy, and no doubt made a friend.

There needs to be a sea-change in the way we feel about others and ourselves...

THE CAUSES OF ILL HEALTH

I am convinced that the root cause of ill health is physical, mental and emotional stress.

National statistics for the UK state that "sharp peaks in mortality occurred around the first world war, when deaths were mainly due to respiratory and infectious diseases." Surely this must have been due to grief and anxiety over the war.

The 'Choice Theory' school of counselling has discovered a link between heart disease and suppressed anger.

Poverty can bring more problems than simply a straitened budget. Being poor arouses feelings of insecurity and fear, which may lead to drug-taking for relief, in a never-ending cycle. The emotional stress could account for the higher incidence of of illness amongst the poor.

Excessive pressure in schools and the workplace can cause a build-up of stress which is damaging to our health. Many young people suffer breakdowns and sometimes commit suicide during their teens or early twenties. Business executives are known to be prone to heart attacks at a relatively early age. Many sole traders and businessmen work too many hours. I feel sure that a survey would show that their physical health can be affected over a period of time. Even athletes and keep-fit fanatics can be at risk from physical stress, and marathon runners sometimes collapse when their bodies can take no more.

Unhappy or broken relationships cause great emotional stress, and victims frequently end up with breakdowns requiring hospital treatment and long periods of convalescence. The family unit has long been the bastion of emotional security, but the erosion of family values has frequently made it a battleground for the sexes and a major obstacle to the health and happiness of countless couples and their children.

Unnatural behaviour may also lead to ill health. AIDS and other sexually-transmitted diseases would surely soon disappear if people followed their hearts instead of their libido. Promiscuity only occurs because people ignore the promptings of 'true love', which comes to everyone around the age of puberty, and would last a lifetime if given the chance.

With regard to the feeding of babies, breast-feeding surely is best, as a child's immune system needs a mother's milk. And there may be less risk of breast cancer, which every woman dreads.

In short, the best recipe for vibrant health is freedom from stress and a natural way of life. True happiness comes with being 'in love' with one's partner, and health goes naturally hand-in-hand with happiness.

HEALTH AND HAPPINESS

Health and happiness go together. I was unhappy as a child, and forever afflicted with heavy colds and violent head-aches, and I didn't sleep well at all. I was ill with anxiety and depression when I was twenty-one, and addicted to alcohol for twenty-five years, a living hell. Later I suffered a heart attack, which my counsellor thought could be due to unexpired anger inside. I know now you need to have LOVE inside to be really happy and well,

The happiest state of all is when you're in love. The sun seems to shine every day, you enjoy every thing you do, and your head and your heels are somewhere up in the clouds. It's the most wonderful feeling there is, and of course you adore the person concerned.

Few appear to have found such love, with 50% of relationships falling apart, and a great many women stranded and insecure, until they can find another man, and living a life without love. I have seen many in mental hospital, and some men as well, recovering from the stress.

National statistics state that "despite increases in life expectancy... the proportion of people reporting a limiting longstanding illness has increased over the last three decades from 15% of adults in 1975 to 20% in 1998-9", and women are more likely than men "to report having problems with their general health and the normal activities of life."

Could it not be that stressful relationships, pressure in schools and the workplace, and the money obsession as well, have a great deal to do with this?

FOOD FOR THOUGHT

I am convinced that people binge on food and become obese because they are unhappy inside. Maybe their relationship isn't working, or perhaps they've been unkind to their kids and are weighed down with guilt inside. Or maybe they live alone, and find consolation in ·eating to excess.

Obsessions take many forms, and I suppose the chief ones are drink, drugs and gambling, which can ruin a person's life. But there are workaholics, fitness fanatics, cleanliness fiends, and of course those who never can get enough sex, to name but a few.

I am certain the problem with all is a lack of love in their sad and sorry lives. Dieticians and health clubs may help with obesity, but many 'have a go' with some success, and then go back to their former weight. There can be no better recipe for success than a happy outlook on life.

Then, I submit, you can eat whatever you like, and you won't put on weight, nor take any harm. The body knows its own needs, and will naturally revolt if given the same regime every day. We know what foods appeal, and are guided by instinct to choose the ones we need.

If that wasn't so, the hospitals would be overwhelmed with cases of malnutrition!!

THERE MUST BE A REASON...

There must be a reason for everything. We sleep because we need rest; we eat and drink to keep us alive, we work because we need food and a home to keep us warm and dry, the sun is needed to keep us warm and to nourish our plants, and without water we would die.

Logical investigation into the reasons why has taught us a great deal about the human form. We know the functions of many of its parts, and how they combine to keep us fit and well. We can also tinker here and there with drugs or operations to make repairs to extend our lives and improve our bodily functions.

We can even produce 'test-tube' babies from basic life ingredients, though we cannot create life as such, and when our 'life force' or spirit has departed when we die, we cannot replace it or bring it back. Life is full of things that give us pleasure. We enjoy having a meal, going for a drive in the car, being with friends, having a pint down the pub, and so on. The list is endless, and many of the things we do are because they give us pleasure. And because life is pleasurable, no-one, apart from some who are terminally ill, would wish to die. Nonetheless no-one would wish to live forever in 'time', which would seem to make sense if Heaven is just round the corner when we die.

Science has uncovered many of the laws which govern material things, yet whenever there is something we don't understand, we assume that chaos reigns, there is no God, and no real reason for anything.

But our earth is still at an early stage, with five billion years to go before the sun expires, so there's plenty of time to discover more of the reasons why!

One thing's for sure, if something happened which God had not intended, then God could not be an allpowerful God after all, which doesn't make any sense. For a God, by definition, can surely do anything, any way, anywhere, whenever He likes. Surely that is God. So everything must be intended, and if so there must be a reason for everything.

AN ALL-KNOWING GOD

A good gardener knows how to grow a good plant from seed. He knows the soil required, the amounts of moisture to apply, and how much light, warmth and air will be needed to achieve success. If he was omniscient he would know precisely when it would flower, the size of the flowers and exactly when they would fade.

One would hardly expect a good gardener to know all that to the point of perfection, but an all-powerful, all-knowing God surely would.

A seed is genetically programmed to produce a particular plant, and the same of course applies to any form of life, including human beings. So surely we can assume that God knows exactly how life is formed, and how it will grow, for every creature there is. And like the gardener He knows the ingredients required for a healthy plant, and for a healthy, happy human being.

For reasons unknown, we seem to be left to ourselves to bring about a peaceful, happy world, if we can, which is surely not an impossible goal.

If that is God's plan, then surely it must come someday, with love as the cornerstone and guiding principle for everything we do.

The gardener loves the plants he grows. He would never put poison down and see them die.

Surely a loving God must feel the same...

THE OTHER SIDE OF THE COIN

A thought or a feeling is an insubstantial thing. It cannot be touched or captured on canvas, although activity can be detected in the brain. But the activity in the brain is not the thought or feeling itself, which is the metaphysical or spiritual side of the coin.

Thoughts and feelings may be communicated by voice and physical gesture. Anger may be reflected in the glare in someone's eyes. Fear, guilt, hurt and love can also be seen in the eyes. But eyes are not the feeling itself, only a vehicle of expression, of which there are many when thoughts and feelings occur.

We also have instincts and natural desires, a whole range of urges demanding our attention as we go through life. We cannot see, touch or measure them, although they are there nonetheless. Hunger and thirst are there to the end, for without them we would die. The sex drive is powerful too, and so is the will to survive. We are propelled by the will to satisfy our natural desires the best way we can, and belief in ourselves plays a very important part. We cannot touch or measure belief, but it is there from the start nonetheless.

We all have a moral consciousness, which guides and directs us in all our affairs, and an awareness of the truth which we always should respect. It is not possible to see or touch our moral consciousness, but we all know it's there nonetheless.

So a human being is much, much more than mere flesh and blood, which is all we discard when we journey on, we surely must hope, to unalloyed bliss in Heaven.

SOMETHING OF VALUE

Nothing has a value unless it is interesting, and what interests one person may not interest another.

We may like a newspaper because of the editorials, or a particular columnist may appeal, or perhaps it's the pin-ups that lure us to buy. But whatever object meets our eye, we turn aside and ignore it if our interest isn't engaged.

Life on earth is certainly interesting, in all its various forms. No two people have the same features, apart from identical twins, throughout the entire world, which is a miracle in itself. No painter would dream of painting the same picture twice. So infinite variety appears to be a principle of creation, and part of the plan for the earth, and perhaps for the wider universe,

Although we all project a good deal, everyone lives in the 'now'. We just don't know what will happen next, at any point in time. No doubt we would be fearful at times and possibly bored if we did. So surprise is an integral part of life, which helps to make it interesting, and thereby enhances its value. A sense of humour, which we all have from birth, is also an asset which enhances life's value enormously!

But nothing can match the joy and the wonder of boygirl relationships when two people are in love. 'True love' is surely the best thing we know, and comes right out of the blue. If we ever have feelings of low self-worth, there is nothing like love to give us a value we never imagined we had, and if God gave us a value, He surely won't take it away...

───────────────

A QUESTION OF TIME

If Heaven is 'timeless' it has no start or end. So if life has to start it has to be started in 'time'. Perhaps time started when the 'big bang' took place, and human beings eventually filled our planet, with all the God-given gifts which seem to make us special not forgetting the importance of all the other flora and fauna which grace the earth.

The world is a beautiful place, with wonderful dawns and sunsets, a huge variety of landscapes and climates, and constant change taking place. Any composer, writer or artist creates because he loves to create, and he loves the products of his genius. He may struggle a little at first, to obtain the perfection he craves, but it all comes right in the end.

So surely God must love His creation too, and perhaps all the pain and suffering are simply the birth-pains of our world, which is still in its early infancy, with plenty of time for improvement in every respect.

There are as many solar systems like ours as there are grains of sand on the earth. Such suffering as our planet has known would surely be unthinkable for all those grains of sand, so perhaps we are living through the birth-pains of the universe itself, and our tiny world is more important than we think!

We live at a time of incessant conflict around the world, and nuclear technology remains a constant threat. But global communications offer a better chance for dialogue than ever before. So perhaps the time has come at last for God to show His love for His creation...

WHICH WAY HEAVEN?

Do the Anglicans go to Heaven and no-one else, the Catholics, Jehovah's Witnesses or Muslims and no-one else? If you don't BELIEVE what happens then? and which one do you CHOOSE from the multitude of faiths around the world?

Pretty delicate matter. Difficult decision. Make the wrong choice and you end up maybe somewhere ELSE??

We know from all the evidence that Christ suffered and died for us on the cross and then went on into Heaven. But was His sacrifice worth it? There are so many denominations of Christianity it must be a hopeless task to strike lucky and pick the right one!

How can an all-powerful, all-loving God fail to forgive a man who is made a monster by malign influences in early life and send him to perdition?? The bible says the "wicked shall perish", but where do you draw the line? How wicked do you need to be, or rather how good to get into Heaven? Or is Heaven the exclusive preserve of a few, who are so saintly in their lives it's the only place they can go- or so they would like to think?

It seems to me there are degrees of 'loving' and being 'good' as well as degrees of being 'wicked' or 'evil', and then sometimes people CHANGE from being evil to being good with God's help, so what becomes of THEM?

The simple truth is we ALL go to Heaven, every man, woman and child that was ever born, and I am certain of THAT as I am of the leaves on the trees, the wind that blows, and the great canopy of the sky above!

WHAT THE WORLD NEEDS NOW...

In an ideal world 'true love' would be taken seriously. Family relationships would be firm and strong. Children would be happy and loved, and none would be left in 'care'. The elderly would be loved and looked after in the family home, with no-one having to live alone. Mental illness would cease to cast its dark shadow over people's lives, as everyone would be happy, and even physical ailments would, I believe, in time disappear.

Pressurised education would come to an end, but standards would leap to undreamed-of heights as children followed their natural aims and aptitudes. Teachers would be more switched on and happy, not having to push or cajole, or fill in voluminous forms. A whole new spirit would come to our schools, with learning a joy and a pleasure for all, no tears, no fear of failure, no breakdowns EVER AGAIN.

Regarding the unemployed, a caring, loving government would strive tooth and nail to find them work. An end would come to tedious forms, as TRUST came back to our world, with everyone having the love at the start. There would be less need for police, as people in work have less incentive to break the law.

With so much love in their hearts, people would take in the homeless off the streets, rather than see them suffer and die.

True love is the key to it all. Who would not wish for a loving, caring world in place of the one we have? Sometime, surely, we must see SENSE and make it all come true.

True love is...

A voice which makes my heart stand still,

A shock of curls my senses fill,

The swish of a skirt, the glance of an eye,

A smile that opens the earth and sky.

Musea King

―――――――――――

Beauty is truth, truth beauty,
that is all ye know on earth
and all ye need to know.

Keats

Printed in Great Britain
by Amazon